TO

_____

FROM

_____

DATE

_____

A PASSION FOR CHRIST

*Jesus answered, "If anyone loves Me,
he will keep My word. My Father will love him,
and We will come to him and make
Our home with him."*

John 14:23 HCSB

Are you passionate about your life, your loved ones, your work, and your Savior? As a believer who has been saved by a risen Christ, you should be.

Why did Christ endure the humiliation and torture of the cross? He did it for you. His love is as near as your next breath, as personal as your next thought, more essential than your next heartbeat. And what must you do in response to the Savior's gifts? You must accept His love, praise His name, and share His message of salvation. And, you must conduct yourself in a manner that demonstrates to all the world that your acquaintance with the Master is not a passing fancy but that it is, instead, the cornerstone and the touchstone of your life.

As a thoughtful Christian, you have every reason to be enthusiastic about life, but sometimes the struggles of everyday living may leave you feeling exhausted or discouraged. If you fear that your passion for life is slowly fading away, it's time to slow down, to rest, to recount your blessings, to worship, and to pray. When you do, God can restore your energy and your faith.

If you allow Christ to reign over your

A PASSION
FOR
CHRIST

A PASSION
FOR
LIFE

Scripture quotations are taken from:

The Holy Bible, King James Version

The Holy Bible, New International Version (NIV) Copyright © 1973, 1978, 1984, by International Bible Society. Used by permission of Zondervan Publishing House. All rights reserved.

The Holy Bible, New King James Version (NKJV) Copyright © 1982 by Thomas Nelson, Inc. Used by permission.

The New American Standard Bible®, (NASB) Copyright © 1960, 1962, 1963, 1968, 1971, 1972, 1973, 1975, 1977, 1995 by The Lockman Foundation. Used by permission.

The Holy Bible, New Living Translation, (NLT) Copyright © 1996. Used by permission of Tyndale House Publishers, Inc., Wheaton, Illinois 60189. All rights reserved.

New Century Version®. (NCV) Copyright   © 1987, 1988, 1991 by Word Publishing, a division of Thomas Nelson, Inc. All rights reserved. Used by permission.

The Message (MSG)- This edition issued by contractual arrangement with NavPress, a division of The Navigators, U.S.A. Originally published by NavPress in English as THE MESSAGE: The Bible in Contemporary Language copyright 2002-2003 by Eugene Peterson. All rights reserved.

The Holman Christian Standard Bible™ (HCSB) Copyright © 1999, 2000, 2001 by Holman Bible Publishers. Used by permission.

Cover Design & Page Layout by Bart Dawson
Copy written and compiled by: Criswell Freeman

ISBN 1-58334-241-9

Printed in the United States of America

TABLE OF CONTENTS

INTRODUCTION

Are you passionate about your God *and* about the life that your God has given you? You most certainly should be. And, are you passionate about the Son of God who sacrificed His life on a cross so that you might have life eternal? The answer to that question will determine the tone, the direction, and the quality of your life.

If you're already an enthusiastic believer who readily shares Christ's message and His love, this text can help keep your enthusiasm high. But perhaps, like many Christians, you are facing struggles that leave you feeling decidedly *unenthusiastic*. If so, this book can help renew your passion for life *and* for Christ.

This text is intended to assist you as you infuse a sense of passion and purpose into every aspect of your life; as such, the book is divided into 31 chapters, one for each day of the month. Each chapter contains Bible verses, a brief essay, inspirational quotations from noted Christian thinkers, and a prayer.

During the next 31 days, please try this experiment: read a chapter each day. If you're already passionate about your faith, your profession, and your world, this book can help you maintain that enthusiasm. But if you lack a certain zest for life—if you feel tired, or discouraged, or both—the ideas on these pages can help you recharge your spiritual batteries *and* refocus your spiritual vision.

Every day provides opportunities to put Jesus where He belongs: at the center of your life. When you worship Him, not just with words, but with deeds, you become a dutiful disciple of Christ. Then, you can share your passion and your faith with a world that needs both.

It was not the soldiers who killed him,
nor the screams of the mob:
It was his devotion to us.

Max Lucado

Dorothy Sayers has said that God underwent
three great humiliations in his efforts to rescue
the human race. The first was the Incarnation,
when he took on the confines of a physical
body. The second was the Cross, when
he suffered the ignominy of public execution.
The third humiliation, Sayers suggested,
is the church. In an awesome act of self-denial,
God entrusted his reputation
to ordinary people.

Philip Yancey

God did not die for man because of some value
He perceived in him. The value of each human
soul considered simply in itself, out of relation
to God, is zero. As St. Paul writes, to have died
for valuable men would have been not divine,
but merely heroic; but God died for sinners.
He loved us not because we were lovable,
but because He is Love.

C. S. Lewis

Keep your eyes on Jesus, who both began and
finished this race we're in. Study how he did it.
Because he never lost sight of where he was headed,
that exhilarating finish in and with God,
he could put up with anything along the way:
cross, shame, whatever. And now he's there,
in the place of honor, right alongside God.

Hebrews 12:2 MSG

TODAY'S PRAYER

Dear Lord, I humbly give thanks for the
sacrifice of my Savior, Jesus Christ. He died
on a cross for me, and He gave His life so that I
might have eternal life. I praise You, Father, for
Your grace, for Your love, and for the priceless
gift of Your Son. May I share the message
of the cross with everyone I meet this day.
Amen

BIBLE VERSES TO CONSIDER

Philippians 2:5-8; Acts 2:23-24;
1 Corinthians 1:17; Galatians 6:14

THE GIFT
OF GRACE

*For by grace you have been saved through faith,
and that not of yourselves; it is the gift of God.*

Ephesians 2:8 NKJV

Christ sacrificed His life on the cross so that we might have life eternal. This gift, freely given from God's only begotten Son, is the priceless possession of everyone who accepts Him as Lord and Savior. Thankfully, grace is not an earthly reward for righteous behavior; it is, instead, a blessed spiritual gift. When we accept Christ into our hearts, we are saved by His grace.

The familiar words from the second chapter of Ephesians make God's promise perfectly clear: we are saved, not by our own good works, but by God's infinite love. In response to this blessing, we must be humble, we must be grateful, and we must be obedient.

God's grace is the ultimate gift, and we owe to Him the ultimate in thanksgiving. Let us praise the Creator for His priceless gift, and let us share the Good News with the world. We return our Father's love by accepting His grace and by sharing His message and His love. When we do, we are eternally blessed. God is waiting patiently for each of us to accept His gift of eternal life. Let us claim Christ's gift today.

The realization that it was impossible to get
into heaven on my own ticket became
a tremendously liberating experience for me.
I realized I had to catch a different train,
and that's when I was run over by
a locomotive called grace.

Bill Hybels

The law tells me how crooked I am.
Grace comes along and straightens me out.

D. L. Moody

The life of faith is a daily exploration of
the constant and countless ways in which
God's grace and love are experienced.

Eugene Peterson

In your greatest weakness, turn to your greatest
strength, Jesus, and hear Him say,
"My grace is sufficient for you,
for My strength is made perfect in weakness"
(2 Corinthians 12:9, NKJV).

Lisa Whelchel

*For God so loved the world that he gave his one
and only Son, that whoever believes in him
shall not perish but have eternal life.*

John 3:16 NIV

TODAY'S PRAYER

Lord, Your grace is a gift that cannot be earned.
It is a gift that was given freely when I accepted
Your Son as my personal Savior. Freely have
I received Your gifts, Father. Let me freely share
my gifts, my possessions, my time, my energy,
and my faith. And let my words, my thoughts,
my prayers, and my deeds bring honor to
You and to Your Son, now and forever.
Amen

BIBLE VERSES TO CONSIDER

*1 Corinthians 15:10; 2 Peter 3:18; Hebrews 4:16;
Romans 3:23-24*

A PASSION
FOR LIFE

*I urge you to live a life worthy
of the calling you have received.*

Ephesians 4:1 NIV

Are you living the triumphant life that God has promised? Or are you, instead, a spiritually shrinking violet? As you ponder that question, consider this: God does not intend that you live a life that is commonplace or mediocre. And He doesn't want you to hide your light "under a basket." Instead, He wants you to "Let your light so shine before men, that they may see your good works and glorify your Father in heaven" (Matthew 5:16 NKJV). In short, God wants you to live a triumphant life so that others might know precisely what it means to be a believer.

If you're a believer whose passion for Christ is evident for all to see, congratulations. But if you're plagued by the temptations and distractions of these troubled times—or if you've allowed the inevitable frustrations of everyday life to obscure the joy that is rightfully yours—it's time to recharge your spiritual batteries.

The Christian life should be a triumphal celebration, a daily exercise in thanksgiving and praise. Join that celebration today. And while you're at it, make sure that you let others know that you've joined.

The Christian life is motivated, not by a list
of do's and don'ts, but by the gracious
outpouring of God's love and blessing.

Anne Graham Lotz

When we invite Jesus into our lives,
we experience life in the fullest,
most vital sense.

Catherine Marshall

The measure of a life, after all,
is not its duration but its donation.

Corrie ten Boom

People, places, and things were never meant to
give us life. God alone is the author
of a fulfilling life.

Gary Smalley & John Trent

My purpose is to give life in all its fullness.

John 10:10 HCSB

TODAY'S PRAYER

Thank You, Father, for the abundant life that is mine through Christ Jesus. Guide me according to Your will, and help me to be a worthy servant through all that I say and do. Give me courage, Lord, to claim the rewards You have promised, and when I do, let all the glory be Yours.

Amen

BIBLE VERSES TO CONSIDER

1 Thessalonians 4:11-12; 1 Timothy 4:16;
2 Corinthians 3:6; 2 Peter 1:3

A PASSIONATE
SENSE
OF PURPOSE

You will show me the path of life;
in Your presence is fullness of joy;
at Your right hand are pleasures forevermore.

Psalm 16:11 NKJV

Life is best lived on purpose, not by accident: the sooner we discover what God intends for us to do with our lives, the better. But God's purposes aren't always clear to us. Sometimes we wander aimlessly in a wilderness of our own making. And sometimes, we struggle mightily against God in a vain effort to find success and happiness through our own means, not His.

Whenever we struggle against God's plans, we suffer. When we resist God's calling, our efforts bear little fruit. Our best strategy, therefore, is to seek God's wisdom and to follow Him wherever He chooses to lead. When we do so, we are blessed.

When we align ourselves with God's purposes, we avail ourselves of His power and His peace. And as we seek to discern God's will, we should do so with a passionate sense of God's possibilities and a quiet trust in God's promises.

Are you earnestly seeking to discern God's purpose for your life? If so, remember this:

1. God has a plan for your life;

2. If you seek that plan sincerely and prayerfully, you will find it;

3. When you discover God's purpose for your life, you will experience abundance, peace, joy, and power—God's power. And that's the only kind of power that really matters.

When we realize and embrace the Lord's will
for us, we will love to do it.
We won't want to do anything else.
It's a passion.

Franklin Graham

Blessed are those who know what on earth
they are here on earth to do and set themselves
about the business of doing it.

Max Lucado

You were made by God and for God—
and until you understand that,
life will not make sense.

Rick Warren

To everything there is a season,
a time for every purpose under heaven.

Ecclesiastes 3:1 NKJV

TODAY'S PRAYER

Dear Lord, I know that You have a purpose
for my life, and I will seek that purpose today
and every day that I live. Let my actions be
pleasing to You, and let me share
Your Good News with a world that so
desperately needs Your healing hand
and the salvation of Your Son.
Amen

BIBLE VERSES TO CONSIDER

Ephesians 4:1; Romans 8:28; Romans 12:6-8;
Psalm 20:4

YOUR
PASSIONATE
TESTIMONY

*For God has not given us a spirit of fear
and timidity, but of power, love, and self-discipline.
So you must never be ashamed to tell others
about our Lord.*

2 Timothy 1:7-8 NLT

In his second letter to Timothy, Paul offers a message to believers of every generation when he writes, "God has not given us a spirit of fear and timidity" (1:7). Paul's meaning is crystal clear: When sharing our testimonies, we, as Christians, must be courageous, forthright, passionate, and unashamed.

We live in a world that desperately needs the healing message of Christ Jesus. Every believer, each in his or her own way, bears responsibility for sharing the Good News of our Savior. It is important to remember that we bear testimony through both words and actions. Wise Christians follow the admonition of St. Francis of Assisi who advised, "Preach the gospel at all times and, if necessary, use words."

If you are a believer in Christ, you know how He has touched your heart and changed your life. Now is the time to share your testimony with others. So today, preach the Gospel through your words and your deeds…but not necessarily in that order.

Every believer may be brought to understand
that the only object of his life is to help
to make Christ King on the earth.

Andrew Murray

One of the deepest pleas Christ made to
His Father on the eve of the Crucifixion is
that His followers would be one. "May they
be brought to complete unity to let the world
know that you sent me and have loved them
even as you have loved me" (John 17:23).
Unity unleashes such a powerful testimony that,
through it, Christ said the world would know
that God sent Him.

Beth Moore

Our faith grows by expression.
If we want to keep our faith, we must share it.
We must act.

Billy Graham

You cannot keep silent once you have
experienced the salvation of Jesus Christ.

Warren Wiersbe

You are a chosen people. You are a kingdom of priests, God's holy nation, his very own possession. This is so you can show others the goodness of God, for he called you out of the darkness into his wonderful light.

1 Peter 2:9 NLT

TODAY'S PRAYER

Dear Lord, the life that I live and the words that I speak bear testimony to my faith. Make me a faithful and passionate servant of Your Son, and let my testimony be worthy of You. Let my words be sure and true, Lord, and let my actions point others to You.
Amen

BIBLE VERSES TO CONSIDER

1 Peter 3:15; Acts 1:8; Luke 12:8-9; Matthew 10:27

A LIFE THAT IS WORTHY

And we pray this in order that you may live
a life worthy of the Lord and may please him
in every way: bearing fruit in every good work,
growing in the knowledge of God.

Colossians 1:10 NIV

As followers of Christ, we must each ask ourselves an important question: "What kind of example am I?" The answer to that question determines, in large part, whether or not we are positive influences on our own little corners of the world.

Are you a believer whose life serves as a powerful example of righteousness? Are you a person whose behavior serves as a positive role model for young people? Are you the kind of Christian whose actions, day in and day out, are based upon integrity, fidelity, and a love for the Lord? If so, you are not only blessed by God, you are also a powerful force for good in a world that desperately needs positive influences such as yours.

Phillips Brooks advised, "Be such a person, and live such a life, that if every person were such as you, and every life a life like yours, this earth would be God's Paradise." And that's sound advice because our families and friends are watching . . . and, for that matter, so is God.

God is the only goal worthy of man's efforts;
the fitting end of human existence is
a loving union with God.

St. Augustine

Our God is the sovereign Creator of
the universe! He loves us as His own children
and has provided every good thing we have;
He is worthy of our praise every moment.

Shirley Dobson

We don't give up. We look up. We trust.
We believe. And our optimism is not hollow.
Christ has proven worthy. He has shown that
he never fails. That's what makes God, God.

Max Lucado

For one man who can introduce another to
Jesus Christ by the way he lives and by
the atmosphere of his life, there are a thousand
who can only talk jargon about him.

Oswald Chambers

Watch ye therefore, and pray always,
that ye may be accounted worthy to escape
all these things that shall come to pass,
and to stand before the Son of man.

Luke 21:36 KJV

TODAY'S PRAYER

Dear Lord, make me a Christian who is worthy
of others' trust. Let me seek the truth and
speak the truth, today and every day of my life.
May Jesus always be the standard for truth in
my life so that I might be a worthy example to
others and a worthy servant to You.
Amen

BIBLE VERSES TO CONSIDER

Philippians 4:8; 1 Thessalonians 2:12;
Matthew 10:38-39; Ephesians 4:1

A PASSIONATE
SENSE OF
TRANSFORMATION

Therefore if anyone is in Christ,
he is a new creature; the old things passed away;
behold, new things have come.

2 Corinthians 5:17 HCSB

God has the power to transform your life if you invite Him to do so. Your decision is straightforward: whether or not to allow the Father's transforming power to work in you and through you. God stands at the door and waits; all you must do is knock. When you do, God always answers.

Sometimes, the demands of daily life may drain you of strength or rob you of the joy that is rightfully yours in Christ. But even on your darkest day, you may be comforted by the knowledge that God has the power to renew your spirit and your life.

Are you in need of a new beginning? If so, turn your heart toward God in prayer. Are you weak or worried? Take the time—or, more accurately, make the time—to delve deeply into God's Holy Word. Are you spiritually depleted? Call upon fellow believers to support you, and call upon God to renew your passion for life. When you do, you'll discover that the Creator of the universe is in the business of making all things new—including you.

In the midst of the pressure and the heat,
I am confident His hand is on my life,
developing my faith until I display His glory,
transforming me into a vessel of honor
that pleases Him!

Anne Graham Lotz

God has sent His Holy Spirit to transform us
into more accurate reflections
of who God is . . . .

Bill Hybels

God's work is not in buildings,
but in transformed lives.

Ruth Bell Graham

God became man to turn creatures into sons:
not simply to produce better men of the old
kind but to produce a new kind of man.

C. S. Lewis

And do not be conformed to this world,
but be transformed by the renewing of your mind,
that you may prove what is that good and acceptable
and perfect will of God.

Romans 12:2 NKJV

TODAY'S PRAYER

Lord, when I accepted Jesus as my personal
Savior, You transformed me forever and made
me whole. Let me passionately share
Your Son's message with my friends,
with my family, and with the world.
You are a God of love, redemption, conversion,
and salvation. I will praise You
today and forever.
Amen

BIBLE VERSES TO CONSIDER

Ezekiel 36:26; Isaiah 43:18-19; Psalm 51:10;
Revelation 21:5

PASSIONATE PRAISE

*I will thank you, L*ord*, with all my heart;*
I will tell of all the marvelous things you have done.
I will be filled with joy because of you.
I will sing praises to your name, O Most High.

Psalm 9:1-2 NLT

When is the best time to praise God? In church? Before dinner is served? When we tuck little children into bed? None of the above. The best time to praise God is all day, every day, to the greatest extent we can, with thanksgiving in our hearts, and with a song on our lips.

Mrs. Charles E. Cowman, the author of the classic devotional text *Streams in the Desert*, wrote, "Two wings are necessary to lift our souls toward God: prayer and praise. Prayer asks. Praise accepts the answer."

Do you sincerely desire to be a worthy servant of the One who has given you eternal love and eternal life? Then praise Him—passionately and purposefully—for who He is and for what He has done for you. And don't just praise Him on Sunday morning. Praise Him all day long, every day, for as long as you live . . . and then for all eternity.

How delightful a teacher, but gentle a provider,
how bountiful a giver is my Father!
Praise, praise to Thee, O manifested Most High.

Jim Elliot

The time for universal praise is sure to come
some day. Let us begin to do our part now.

Hannah Whitall Smith

I am to praise God for all things, regardless of
where they seem to originate. Doing this is
the key to receiving the blessings of God.
Praise will wash away my resentments.

Catherine Marshall

Be not afraid of saying too much in
the praises of God;
all the danger is of saying too little.

Matthew Henry

Is anyone happy? Let him sing songs of praise.

James 5:13 NIV

TODAY'S PRAYER

Dear Lord, I will praise You today and
every day that I live. And, I will praise
Your Son, the Savior of my life. Christ's love is
boundless and eternal. Let my thoughts,
my prayers, my words, and my deeds praise
Him now and forever.
Amen

BIBLE VERSES TO CONSIDER

*Psalm 100:4-5; Psalm 106:1;
Philippians 2:10-11; Hebrews 13:15*

SHARING YOUR BURDENS WITH GOD

*Cast your burden upon the LORD and
He will sustain you: He will never allow
the righteous to be shaken.*

Psalm 55:22 NASB

The Bible promises this: tough times are temporary but God's love is not—God's love endures forever. So what does that mean to you? Just this: From time to time, everybody faces hardships and disappointments, and so will you. And when tough times arrive, God *always* stands ready to protect you and to heal you. Your task is straightforward: you must share your burdens with Him.

As Corrie ten Boom observed, "Any concern that is too small to be turned into a prayer is too small to be made into a burden." Those are comforting words, especially in these difficult days.

Whatever the size of your challenges, God is big enough to handle them. Ask for His help today, with faith and with fervor. Instead of turning things over in your mind, turn them over to God in prayer. Instead of worrying about your next decision, ask God to lead the way. Cast your burdens upon the One who cannot be shaken, and rest assured that He *always* hears your prayers.

God delights in the prayers of His children—
prayers that express our love for Him,
prayers that share our deepest burdens
with Him.

Billy Graham

Jesus is calling the weary to rest,
Calling today, calling today,
Bring Him your burden and you shall be blest;
He will not turn you away.

Fanny Crosby

We look at our burdens and heavy loads, and
we shrink from them. But, if we lift them and
bind them about our hearts, they become wings,
and on them we can rise and soar toward God.

Mrs. Charles E. Cowman

No matter how heavy the burden, daily strength
is given, so I expect we need not give ourselves
any concern as to what the outcome will be.
We must simply go forward.

Annie Armstrong

Come to Me, all you who are weary and burdened, and I will give you rest. Take My yoke upon you and learn from Me, because I am gentle and humble in heart, and you will find rest for your souls. For My yoke is easy and My burden is light.

Matthew 11:28-30 HCSB

TODAY'S PRAYER

Dear Lord, whatever "it" is, You can handle it! Let me turn to You when I am burdened and when I am worried. You are my loving Father, and I will always trust you.

Amen

BIBLE VERSES TO CONSIDER

2 Corinthians 1:8-10; Psalm 146:8; Galatians 6:2; Matthew 6:33-34

PASSIONATE
SERVICE

The greatest among you must be a servant.
But those who exalt themselves will be humbled,
and those who humble themselves will be exalted.

Matthew 23:11-12 NLT

The teachings of Jesus are clear: We achieve greatness through passionate, unselfish service to others. But, as weak human beings, we sometimes fall short as we seek to puff ourselves up and glorify our own accomplishments. Jesus commands otherwise. He teaches us that the most esteemed men and women are not the self-congratulatory leaders of society but are instead the humblest of servants.

Today, you may feel the temptation to build yourself up in the eyes of your neighbors. Resist that temptation. Instead, serve your neighbors quietly and without fanfare. Find a need and fill it . . . humbly. Lend a helping hand and share a word of kindness . . . anonymously, for this is God's way.

As a humble servant, you will glorify yourself not before men, but before God, and that's what God intends. After all, earthly glory is fleeting: here today and all too soon gone. But, heavenly glory endures throughout eternity. So, the choice is yours: Either you can lift yourself up here on earth and be humbled in heaven, or vice versa. Choose vice versa.

If you aren't serving, you're just existing,
because life is meant for ministry.

Rick Warren

Employ whatever God has entrusted you with,
in doing good, all possible good,
in every possible kind and degree.

John Wesley

In the very place where God has put us,
whatever its limitations, whatever kind of work
it may be, we may indeed serve the Lord Christ.

Elisabeth Elliot

In Jesus, the service of God and the service of
the least of the brethren were one.

Dietrich Bonhoeffer

There are different kinds of gifts, but they are all from the same Spirit. There are different ways to serve but the same Lord to serve.

1 Corinthians 12:4-5 NCV

TODAY'S PRAYER

Lord, You have promised me a life of abundance and joy through Your Son Jesus. Thank You, Lord, for Your blessings, and guide me according to Your will, so that I might be a worthy servant in all that I say and do, this day and everyday.

Amen

BIBLE VERSES TO CONSIDER

1 Peter 1:13; Hebrews 12:28; John 12:26; Philippians 2:5-8

EXPECTING GOD'S MIRACLES

For with God nothing will be impossible.

Luke 1:37 NKJV

Do you expect a miracle today? If you trust the promises of the Bible, you should. And do you believe in an all-powerful God who can do miraculous things *in* you and *through* you? If you're a believer who's been transformed by the love of Christ, you should. But perhaps, as you have faced the inevitable struggles of life here on earth, you have—without realizing it—placed limitations on God. To do so is a profound mistake. God's power has no such limitations, and He can work mighty miracles in your own life if you let Him.

Do you lack a firm faith in God's power to perform miracles for you and your loved ones? If so, you are attempting to place limitations on a God who has none. Instead of doubting your Heavenly Father, you must place yourself in His hands. Instead of doubting God's power, you must trust it. Expect Him to work miracles, and be watchful. With God, absolutely nothing is impossible, including an amazing assortment of miracles that He stands ready, willing, and perfectly able to perform for you and yours.

Too many Christians live below
the miracle level.

Vance Havner

Are you looking for a miracle?
If you keep your eyes wide open and
trust in God, you won't have to look very far.

Marie T. Freeman

Faith means believing in realities that go
beyond sense and sight. It is the awareness of
unseen divine realities all around you.

Joni Eareckson Tada

I could go through this day oblivious to
the miracles all around me or
I could tune in and "enjoy."

Gloria Gaither

*But as it is written: "Eye has not seen,
nor ear heard, nor have entered into the heart of
man the things which God has prepared
for those who love Him."*

1 Corinthians 2:9 NKJV

TODAY'S PRAYER

Heavenly Father, You are the miracle worker of
life; let me trust in Your power and Your love.
With You, Father, all things are possible.
Keep me mindful that You are a God of power
and possibilities, and let me never place
limitations upon You, the Designer
and Creator of the Universe.
Amen

BIBLE VERSES TO CONSIDER

*Hebrews 2:4; John 10:32; Psalm 77:14;
Mark 10:27*

A PASSION
FOR GOD'S
WORD

*For the word of God is living and effective
and sharper than any two-edged sword, penetrating
as far as to divide soul, spirit, joints, and marrow;
it is a judge of the ideas and thoughts of the heart.*

Hebrews 4:12 HCSB

Have you established a passionate relationship with God's Holy Word? Hopefully so. After all, the Bible is unlike any other book; it is a roadmap for life here on earth *and* for life eternal. And, as a believer who has been touched by God's grace, you are called upon to study God's Holy Word, to trust His Word, to follow His commandments, and to share His Good News with the world.

The words of Matthew 4:4 remind us that, "Man shall not live by bread alone but by every word that proceedeth out of the mouth of God" (KJV). As believers, we must study the Bible and meditate upon its meaning for our lives. Otherwise, we deprive ourselves of a priceless gift from our Creator.

Martin Luther observed, "The Bible is alive, it speaks to me; it has feet, it runs after me; it has hands, it lays hold of me. The Bible is not antique or modern. It is eternal." God's Holy Word is, indeed, an eternal, transforming, one-of-a-kind treasure. And, a passing acquaintance with the Good Book is insufficient for Christians who seek to obey God's Word and to understand His will—passionate believers must *never* live by bread alone . . .

Walking in faith brings you to
the Word of God. There you will be healed,
cleansed, fed, nurtured, equipped, and matured.

Kay Arthur

You should not believe your conscience and
your feelings more than the word which
the Lord who receives sinners preaches to you.

Martin Luther

The only way we can understand the Bible is by
personal contact with the Living Word.

Oswald Chambers

There is no way to draw closer to God unless
you are in the Word of God every day.
It's your compass. Your guide.
You can't get where you need to go without it.

Stormie Omartian

All Scripture is given by inspiration of God,
and is profitable for doctrine, for reproof,
for correction, for instruction in righteousness.

2 Timothy 3:16 KJV

TODAY'S PRAYER

Heavenly Father, Your Holy Word is
a light unto the world; let me study it, trust it,
and share it with those who cross my path.
In all that I do, help me be a worthy witness for
You as I share the Good News of
Your perfect Son and Your perfect Word.
Amen

BIBLE VERSES TO CONSIDER

Isaiah 55:10-11; John 14:23; Luke 6:47-48;
Matthew 4:4

PASSIONATE
DISCIPLESHIP

Then He said to them all, "If anyone desires to come after Me, let him deny himself, and take up his cross daily, and follow Me. For whoever desires to save his life will lose it, but whoever loses his life for My sake will save it."

Luke 9:23-24 NKJV

When we have been saved by Christ, we can, if we choose, become passive Christians. We can sit back, secure in our own salvation, and let other believers spread the healing message of Jesus. But to do so is wrong. Instead, we are commanded to become passionate disciples of the One who has saved us, and to do otherwise is a sin of omission with terrible consequences.

When Jesus addressed His disciples, He warned them that each one must, "take up his cross daily and follow me" (Luke 9:23 NIV). Christ's message was clear: in order to follow Him, Christ's disciples must deny themselves and, instead, trust Him completely. Nothing has changed since then.

If we are to be disciples of Christ, we must trust Him and place Him at the very center of our beings. Jesus never comes "next." He is always first. The wonderful paradox, of course, is that it is only by sacrificing ourselves to Him that we gain eternal salvation.

Do you seek to follow Christ? Then pick up His cross today and every day that you live. When you do, He will bless you now and forever.

It is the secret of true discipleship to bear the cross, to acknowledge the death sentence that has been passed on self, and to deny any right that self has to rule over us.

Andrew Murray

Discipleship usually brings us into the necessity of choice between duty and desire.

Elisabeth Elliot

Christian discipleship is a process of paying more and more attention to God's righteousness and less and less attention to our own; finding the meaning of our lives not by probing our moods and motives and morals, but by believing in God's will and purposes; making a map of the faithfulness of God, not charting the rise and fall of our enthusiasms.

Eugene Peterson

There is not Christianity without a cross, for you cannot be a disciple of Jesus without taking up your cross.

Henry Blackaby

Therefore go and make disciples of all nations,
baptizing them in the name of the Father and of
the Son and of the Holy Spirit, and teaching them to
obey everything I have commanded you. And surely
I am with you always, to the very end of the age.

Matthew 28:19-20 NIV

TODAY'S PRAYER

Dear Lord, thank You for the gift of
Your Son Jesus, my personal Savior. Let me be
a worthy disciple of Christ, and let me be ever
grateful for His love. I offer my life to You,
Lord, so that I might live with passion and
with purpose. I will praise You always as
I give thanks for Your Son and
for Your everlasting love.
Amen

BIBLE VERSES TO CONSIDER

John 13:34-35; Matthew 9:37; Ephesians 5:1;
Micah 6:8

THE POWER OF GOD'S PROMISES

Let us hold on to the confession of our hope
without wavering, for He who promised is faithful.

Hebrews 10:23 HCSB

What do you expect from the day ahead? Are you standing on the promises of God? Are you expecting God to do wonderful things, or are you living beneath a cloud of apprehension and doubt? The familiar words of Psalm 118:24 remind us of a profound yet simple truth: "This is the day which the LORD hath made; we will rejoice and be glad in it" (KJV).

For passionate believers, every day begins and ends with God's Son and God's promises. When we accept Christ into our hearts, God promises us the opportunity for earthly peace and spiritual abundance. But more importantly, God promises us the priceless gift of eternal life.

As we face the inevitable challenges of life here on earth, we must arm ourselves with the promises of God's Holy Word. When we do, we can expect the best, not only for the day ahead, but also for all eternity.

The stars may fall, but God's promises will stand and be fulfilled.

J. I. Packer

There are four words I wish we would never forget, and they are, "God keeps his word."

Charles Swindoll

We cannot rely on God's promises without obeying his commandments.

John Calvin

No one who has ever set out to test God's promises fairly, thoroughly, and humbly has ever had to report that God's promises don't work. On the contrary, given a fair opportunity, God always surprises and overwhelms those who truly seek His bounty and His power.

Peter Marshall

For you have need of endurance,
so that when you have done the will of God,
you may receive what was promised.

Hebrews 10:36 NASB

TODAY'S PRAYER

Dear God, the Bible contains many promises.
Let me trust Your promises, and let me live
according to Your Holy Word,
not just for today, but forever.
Amen

BIBLE VERSES TO CONSIDER

Psalm 18:30; Hebrews 6:11-12; Galatians 3:14;
Romans 4:21

FAITH, NOT FEAR

He replied, "You of little faith,
why are you so afraid?" Then he got up
and rebuked the winds and the waves,
and it was completely calm.

Matthew 8:26 NIV

When we trust God, we should trust Him without reservation. But sometimes, especially during life's darker days, trusting God may be difficult. Yet this much is certain: whatever our circumstances, we must continue to plant the seeds of faith in our hearts, trusting that in time God will bring forth a bountiful harvest. Planting the seeds for that harvest requires work, which is perfectly okay with God. After all, He never gives us burdens that we cannot bear.

It is important to remember that the work required to build and sustain our faith is an ongoing process. Corrie ten Boom advised, "Be filled with the Holy Spirit; join a church where the members believe the Bible and know the Lord; seek the fellowship of other Christians; learn and be nourished by God's Word and His many promises. Conversion is not the end of your journey—it is only the beginning."

The work of nourishing *your* faith can and should be joyful work. The hours that you invest in Bible study, prayer, meditation, and worship should be times of enrichment and celebration. And, as you continue to build your life upon a foundation of faith, you will discover that the journey toward spiritual maturity lasts a lifetime. As a child of God, you are never fully "grown": instead, you can continue "growing up" every day of your life. And that's exactly what God wants you to do.

To fear and not be afraid,
that is the paradox of faith.

A. W. Tozer

Fear knocked at the door. Faith answered.
No one was there.

Anonymous

Faith is stronger than fear.

John Maxwell

Faith in God is a terrific venture in the dark.

Oswald Chambers

Fear thou not; for I am with thee.

Isaiah 41:10 KJV

TODAY'S PRAYER

Dear God, sometimes this world can be
a fearful place, full of uncertainty and doubt.
In those dark moments, help me to remember
that You are always near and that You can
overcome any challenge. Give me faith and
let me remember always that with Your love
and Your power, I can live courageously
and faithfully today and every day.
Amen

BIBLE VERSES TO CONSIDER

*Matthew 14:27; Psalm 31:24; 2 Corinthians 5:7;
Hebrews 12:1-2*

A PASSION
FOR ONE'S
PROFESSION

Whatever you do, work at it with all your heart,
as working for the Lord, not for men . . . .

Colossians 3:23 NIV

The old adage is both familiar and true: We must pray as if everything depended upon God, but work as if everything depended upon us. Yet sometimes, when we are weary and discouraged, we may allow our worries to sap our energy and our hope. God has other intentions. God intends that we pray for things, and He intends that we be willing to work for the things that we pray for. More importantly, God intends that *our* work should become *His* work.

Whether you're in school or in the workplace, your success will depend, in large part, upon the passion that you bring to your work. God has created a world in which diligence is rewarded and sloth is not. So whatever you choose to do, do it with commitment, with excitement, with enthusiasm, and with vigor.

God did not create you for a life of mediocrity; He created you for far greater things. Reaching for greater things usually requires work and lots of it, which is perfectly fine with God. After all, He knows that you're up to the task, and He has big plans for you. Very big plans . . .

If our children saw us doing "heartily as unto the Lord" all the work we do, they would learn true happiness. Instead of feeling that they must be allowed to do what they like, they would learn to like what they do.

Elisabeth Elliot

Great relief and satisfaction can come from seeking God's priorities for us in each season, discerning what is "best" in the midst of many noble opportunities, and pouring our most excellent energies into those things.

Beth Moore

We must *trust* as if it all depended on God and *work* as if it all depended on us.

C. H. Spurgeon

It may be that the day of judgment will dawn tomorrow; in that case, we shall gladly stop working for a better tomorrow. But not before.

Dietrich Bonhoeffer

*Each will receive his own reward according
to his own labor . . . . Each man's work
will become evident.*

1 Corinthians 3:8, 13 NASB

TODAY'S PRAYER

Dear Lord, make my work pleasing to You.
Help me to sow the seeds of Your abundance
everywhere I go. Let me be passionate in
all my undertakings and give me patience to
wait for Your harvest.
Amen

BIBLE VERSES TO CONSIDER

*1 Thessalonians 4:11-12; 1 Timothy 5:8;
2 Chronicles 15:7; 2 Timothy 2:15*

PASSIONATE PRAYER

Rejoice always! Pray constantly.
Give thanks in everything,
for this is God's will for you in Christ Jesus.

1 Thessalonians 5:16-18 HCSB

Are you a prayer warrior or have you retreated from God's battlefield? Do you pray about almost everything or about almost nothing? Do you pray constantly and passionately about every aspect of your life, or are you simply satisfied to offer up a few words to God on Sunday morning? The answer to these questions will determine, to a surprising extent, the degree to which God will use you for the glory of His kingdom.

Too many of us, even well-intentioned believers, tend to "compartmentalize" our waking hours into a few familiar categories: work, rest, play, family time, and worship. To do so is a mistake. Worship and prayer should be woven into the fabric of everything we do; they should never be relegated to a weekly one-hour visit to church on Sunday morning.

Theologian Wayne Oates once admitted, "Many of my prayers are made with my eyes open. You see, it seems I'm always praying about something, and it's not always convenient—or safe—to close my eyes." Dr. Oates understood that God always hears our prayers and that the relative position of our eyelids is of no concern to Him.

Today, find a little more time to lift your genuine concerns to God in prayer. And while you're at it, praise Him for all that He has done. Whether your eyes are open or closed, He's listening.

Prayer does not change God; it changes me.

C. S. Lewis

A demanding spirit, with self-will as its rudder, blocks prayer. Prayer is men cooperating with God in bringing from heaven to earth His wondrously good plans for us.

Catherine Marshall

Prayer is the most important tool for your mission to the world. People may refuse our love or reject our message, but they are defenseless against our prayers.

Rick Warren

If my people who are called by my name,
will humble themselves and pray and seek my face
and turn from their wicked ways, then will I hear
from heaven and will forgive their sin
and will heal their land.

2 Chronicles 7:14 NIV

TODAY'S PRAYER

Dear Lord, Your Holy Word commands me to pray without ceasing. Let me take everything to You in prayer. When I am discouraged, let me pray. When I am lonely, let me take my sorrows to You. When I grieve, let me take my tears to You, Father, in prayer. And when I am joyful, let me offer up prayers of thanksgiving.
In all things great and small, at all times, whether happy or sad, let me seek Your wisdom and Your grace . . . in prayer.
Amen

BIBLE VERSES TO CONSIDER

Acts 4:31; James 5:13; Jeremiah 29:11-12;
Luke 18:1

PASSION
AND
ENTHUSIASM

For God has not given us a spirit of fearfulness,
but one of power, love, and sound judgment.

2 Timothy 1:7 HCSB

Can you honestly say that you are an enthusiastic believer? Are you passionate about your faith and excited about your path? Hopefully so. But if your zest for life has waned, it is now time to redirect your efforts and recharge your spiritual batteries. And that means refocusing your priorities by putting God first.

Nothing is more important than your wholehearted commitment to your Creator *and* to His only begotten Son. Your faith must never be an afterthought; it must be your ultimate priority, your ultimate possession, and your ultimate passion.

You are the recipient of Christ's sacrificial love. Accept it enthusiastically and share it passionately. Jesus deserves your enthusiasm; the world deserves it; and you deserve the experience of sharing it.

Catch on fire with enthusiasm and people will
come for miles to watch you burn.

John Wesley

Wherever you are, be all there.
Live to the hilt every situation you believe
to be the will of God.

Jim Elliot

When the dream of our heart is one that God
has planted there, a strange happiness flows
into us. At that moment, all of the spiritual
resources of the universe are released to
help us. Our praying is then at one with
the will of God and becomes a channel for
the Creator's purposes for us and our world.

Catherine Marshall

Don't take hold of a thing unless you want
that thing to take hold of you.

E. Stanley Jones

Do your work with enthusiasm.
Work as if you were serving the Lord,
not as if you were serving only men and women.

Ephesians 6:7 NCV

TODAY'S PRAYER

Dear Lord, You can make all things new.
I am a new creature in Christ Jesus, and when
I fall short in my commitment, You can renew
my effort and my enthusiasm. When I am weak
or worried, restore my strength, Lord,
for my own sake and for the sake
of Your kingdom.
Amen

BIBLE VERSES TO CONSIDER

Colossians 3:23; Romans 12:11;
2 Chronicles 31:21; Ecclesiastes 9:10

IN THE
PRESENCE OF
THE FATHER

Be still, and know that I am God . . . .

Psalm 46:10 KJV

Since God is everywhere, we are free to sense His presence whenever we take the time to quiet our souls and turn our prayers to Him. But sometimes, amid the incessant demands of everyday life, we turn our thoughts far from God; when we do, we suffer.

Do you set aside quiet moments each day to offer praise to your Creator? You should. During these moments of stillness, you will often sense the infinite love and power of our Lord.

The familiar words of Psalm 46:10 remind us to "Be still, and know that I am God." When we do so, we encounter the awesome presence of our loving Heavenly Father, and we are comforted in the knowledge that God is not just near. He is here.

God is at work; He is in full control;
He is in the midst of whatever has happened,
is happening, and will happen.

Charles Swindoll

Oh! what a Savior, gracious to all,
Oh! how His blessings round us fall,
Gently to comfort, kindly to cheer,
Sleeping or waking, God is near.

Fanny Crosby

God walks with us. He scoops us up in His arms
or simply sits with us in silent strength until
we cannot avoid the awesome recognition
that yes, even now, He is here.

Gloria Gaither

The next time you hear a baby laugh or
see an ocean wave, take note.
Pause and listen as his Majesty whispers
ever so gently, "I'm here."

Max Lucado

Be strong and courageous!
Do not tremble or be dismayed, for the LORD
your God is with you wherever you go.

Joshua 1:9 NASB

TODAY'S PRAYER

Heavenly Father, help me to feel Your presence
in every situation and every circumstance.
You are with me, Lord, in times of celebration
and in times of sorrow. You are with me when
I am strong and when I am weak. You never
leave my side even when it seems to me that
You are far away. Today and every day,
God, let me feel You and acknowledge
Your presence so that others, too,
might know You through me.
Amen

BIBLE VERSES TO CONSIDER

2 Chronicles 16:9; Acts 17:27; Isaiah 41:10;
Matthew 18:20

THE POWER
OF
FORGIVENESS

Be gentle with one another, sensitive.
Forgive one another as quickly and thoroughly
as God in Christ forgave you.

Ephesians 4:32 MSG

Bitterness saps your energy; genuine forgiveness renews your spirit. If you find yourself tired, discouraged, or worse, perhaps you need to tap in to the power of forgiveness—perhaps you need to ask God to help you forgive others (just as He has already forgiven you).

God intends that His children lead joyous lives filled with abundance and peace. But sometimes, abundance and peace seem very far away. It is during these darker moments that we must turn to God for the kind of strength that *only* He can give.

Are you embittered about the past? Turn your heart toward God in prayer. Are you spiritually depleted? Call upon fellow believers to encourage you, and call upon Christ to renew your spirit and your life. Do you sincerely want to forgive someone? Ask God to heal your heart. Your goal should be simple: to forgive and to move on. Why? Because the person who hurt you may indeed need your forgiveness, but the one who benefits *most* from your forgiveness is you.

If Jesus forgave those who nailed Him to
the Cross, and if God forgives you and me,
how can you withhold your forgiveness
from someone else?

Anne Graham Lotz

Our relationships with other people are of
primary importance to God.
Because God is love, He cannot tolerate
any unforgiveness or hardness in us toward
any individual.

Catherine Marshall

I firmly believe a great many prayers are
not answered because we are not willing to
forgive someone.

D. L. Moody

Every time we forgive others,
deserving it or not,
we have a reminder of God's forgiveness.

Franklin Graham

Do not judge, and you will not be judged.
Do not condemn, and you will not be condemned.
Forgive, and you will be forgiven.

Luke 6:37 HCSB

TODAY'S PRAYER

Heavenly Father, sometimes I am tempted to
strike out at those who have hurt me.
Keep me mindful that forgiveness is
Your commandment. You have forgiven me,
Lord; let me show my thankfulness to You by
offering forgiveness to others. And, when I do,
may others see Your love reflected
through my words and deeds.
Amen

BIBLE VERSES TO CONSIDER

Mark 11:25; Matthew 18:21-22;
Matthew 7:3-5; Romans 12:19

A PASSIONATE SENSE OF WORSHIP

I was glad when they said to me,
"Let us go to the house of the LORD."

Psalm 122:1 NLT

All of mankind is engaged in worship . . . of one kind or another. The question is not whether we worship, but what we worship. Some of us choose to worship God. The result is a plentiful harvest of joy, peace, and abundance. Others distance themselves from God by foolishly worshiping things of this earth such as fame, fortune, or personal gratification. To do so is a terrible mistake with eternal consequences.

Whenever we place our love for material possessions above our love for God—or when we yield to the countless temptations of this world—we find ourselves engaged in a struggle between good and evil, a clash between God and Satan. Our responses to these struggles have implications that echo throughout our families and throughout our communities.

How can we ensure that we cast our lot with God? We do so, in part, by the practice of regular, purposeful, passionate worship. When we worship God faithfully and fervently, we are blessed. When we fail to worship God, for whatever reason, we forfeit the spiritual gifts that He intends for us.

We must worship our heavenly Father, not just with our words, but also with deeds. We must honor Him, praise Him, and obey Him. As we seek to find purpose and meaning for our lives, we must first seek His purpose and His will. For believers, God comes first. Always first.

It's our privilege to not only raise our hands in worship but also to combine the visible with the invisible in a rising stream of praise and adoration sent directly to our Father.

Shirley Dobson

Passive worship is an oxymoron.

Rick Warren

In Biblical worship you do not find the repetition of a phrase; instead, you find the worshipers rehearsing the character of God and His ways, reminding Him of His faithfulness and His wonderful promises.

Kay Arthur

A time is coming and has now come when
the true worshipers will worship the Father in spirit
and truth, for they are the kind of worshipers
the Father seeks. God is spirit, and his worshipers
must worship in spirit and in truth.

John 4:23-24 NIV

TODAY'S PRAYER

When I worship You, Dear Lord,
You set my path—and my heart—straight.
Let this day and every day be a time of worship.
Whether I am in Your house or simply going
about my daily activities, let me worship You,
not only with words and deeds, but also with
my heart. In the quiet moments of the day,
I will praise You for creating me, loving me,
guiding me, and saving me.
Amen

BIBLE VERSES TO CONSIDER

Matthew 4:10; Philippians 2:9-11;
Psalm 100:1-2; Psalm 66:4

LIVING
COURAGEOUSLY

Be strong and courageous, and do the work.
Don't be afraid or discouraged by the size of
*the task, for the L*ORD *God, my God, is with you.*
He will not fail you or forsake you.

1 Chronicles 28:20 NLT

Every human life is a tapestry of events: some grand, some not-so-grand, and some downright disappointing. When we reach the mountaintops of life, praising God is easy. In the moment of triumph, we trust God's plan. But, when the storm clouds form overhead and we find ourselves in the dark valley of despair, our faith is stretched, sometimes to the breaking point. As Christians, we can be comforted: Wherever we find ourselves, whether at the top of the mountain or the depths of the valley, God is there, and because He cares for us, we can live courageously.

Believing Christians have every reason to be courageous. After all, the ultimate battle has already been fought and won on the cross at Calvary. But, even dedicated followers of Christ may find their courage tested by the inevitable disappointments and tragedies that occur in the lives of believers and non-believers alike.

The next time you find your courage tested to the limit, remember that God is as near as your next breath, and remember that He offers salvation to His children. He is your shield and your strength; He is your protector and your deliverer. Call upon Him in your hour of need and then be comforted. Whatever your challenge, whatever your trouble, God can handle it. And will.

Seeing that a Pilot steers the ship in which we sail, who will never allow us to perish even in the midst of shipwrecks, there is no reason why our minds should be overwhelmed with fear and overcome with weariness.

John Calvin

The great paralysis of our heart is unbelief.

Oswald Chambers

Why rely on yourself and fall?
Cast yourself upon His arm. Be not afraid.
He will not let you slip. Cast yourself
in confidence. He will receive you and heal you.

St. Augustine

The LORD himself goes before you and will be with you; he will never leave you nor forsake you. Do not be afraid; do not be discouraged.

Deuteronomy 31:8 NIV

TODAY'S PRAYER

Lord, sometimes I face challenges that leave me breathless. When I am fearful, let me lean upon You. Keep me ever mindful, Lord, that You are my God, my strength, and my shield. With You by my side, I have nothing to fear. And, with Your Son Jesus as my Savior, I have received the priceless gift of eternal life. Help me to be a grateful and courageous servant this day and every day.
Amen

BIBLE VERSES TO CONSIDER

Genesis 15:1; John 14:27; Matthew 8:26-27; Philippians 4:13

COMPASSION
FOR OTHERS

Finally, all of you be of one mind,
having compassion for one another;
love as brothers, be tenderhearted, be courteous.

1 Peter 3:8 NKJV

God's Word commands us to be compassionate, generous servants to those who need our support. As believers, we have been richly blessed by our Creator. We, in turn, are called to share our gifts, our possessions, our testimonies, and our talents.

Concentration camp survivor Corrie ten Boom correctly observed, "The measure of a life is not its duration but its donation." These words remind us that the quality of our lives is determined not by what we are able to take *from* others, but instead by what we are able to share *with* others.

The thread of compassion is woven into the very fabric of Christ's teachings. If we are to be disciples of Christ, we, too, must be zealous in caring for others. Our Savior expects no less from us. And He deserves no less.

Our Lord worked with people as they were,
and He was patient—not tolerant of sin,
but compassionate.

Vance Havner

When action-oriented compassion is absent,
it's a tell-tale sign that something's
spiritually amiss.

Bill Hybels

We must learn to regard people less in
the light of what they do or do not do,
and more in the light of what they suffer.

Dietrich Bonhoeffer

People don't care how much you know
until they know how much you care.

John Maxwell

Let's see how inventive we can be in
encouraging love and helping out,
not avoiding worshipping together as some do
but spurring each other on.

Hebrews 10:24-25 MSG

TODAY'S PRAYER

Lord, make me a loving, encouraging,
compassionate Christian. And, let my love
for Christ be reflected through the kindness
that I show to my family, to my friends,
and to all who need the healing touch
of the Master's hand.
Amen

BIBLE VERSES TO CONSIDER

Colossians 3:12; Philippians 1:9; Zechariah 7:9;
Ephesians 4:31-32

THE HUMBLE SPIRIT

*And he said to them: "I tell you the truth,
unless you change and become like little children,
you will never enter the kingdom of heaven.
Therefore, whoever humbles himself like
this child is the greatest in heaven."*

Matthew 18:3-4 NIV

Dietrich Bonhoeffer observed, "It is very easy to overestimate the importance of our own achievements in comparison with what we owe others." How true. Even those of us who consider ourselves "self-made" men and women are deeply indebted to more people than we can count. Our first and greatest indebtedness, of course, is to God and His only begotten Son. But we are also indebted to ancestors, parents, teachers, friends, spouses, family members, coworkers, fellow believers . . . and the list goes on.

With so many people who rightfully deserve to share the credit for our successes, how can we gloat? The answer, of course, is that we should not. Proverbs 16:18 warns us that "Pride goes before destruction . . . " (NIV). And 1 Peter 5:5 teaches us that "God opposes the proud but gives grace to the humble" (NIV).

So the next time you're tempted to stick out your chest and say, "Look at me!", resist that temptation. Instead of glorifying your own works, give credit where credit is due, starting with God. And rest assured: There is no such thing as a self-made man. All of us are made by God . . . and He deserves the glory, not us.

If you know who you are in Christ,
your personal ego is not an issue.

Beth Moore

Humility is the fairest and rarest
flower that blooms.

Charles Swindoll

Humility is an attitude.
The Lord is high and lifted up, and we
are supposed to take a position of lowliness.

Franklin Graham

A humble heart is like a magnet that draws
the favor of God toward us.

Jim Cymbala

Humble yourselves therefore under the mighty hand of God, that he may exalt you in due time.

1 Peter 5:6 KJV

TODAY'S PRAYER

Heavenly Father, it is the nature of mankind to be prideful, and I am no exception. When I am boastful, Lord, keep me mindful that all my gifts come from You. When I feel prideful, remind me that You sent Your Son to be a humble carpenter and that Jesus was ridiculed and crucified on a cross. Let me grow beyond my need for earthly praise, God, and let me look only to You for approval.
You are the Giver of all things good;
let me give all the glory to You.
Amen

BIBLE VERSES TO CONSIDER

2 Chronicles 7:14; Isaiah 66:2; James 4:10; Micah 6:8

PASSIONATELY USING GOD'S GIFTS

*We have different gifts, according to the grace given
us. If a man's gift is prophesying, let him use it in
proportion to his faith. . . . if it is teaching, let him
teach; if it is encouraging, let him encourage; . . .
if it is leadership, let him govern diligently;
if it is showing mercy, let him do it cheerfully.*

Romans 12:6-8 NIV

Are you passionately engaged in life? And are you diligently using the tools and talents that God has given you? Hopefully so. After all, the best way to thank God for His gifts is to use them for the glory of His kingdom.

God has given you talents and opportunities that are uniquely yours. Are you willing to use your gifts in the way that God intends? And are you willing to summon the discipline that is required to develop your talents and to hone your skills? That's precisely what God wants you to do, and that's precisely what you should desire for yourself.

As you seek to expand your talents, you will undoubtedly encounter stumbling blocks along the way, such as the fear of rejection or the fear of failure. When you do, don't stumble! Just continue to refine your skills, and offer your services to God. And when the time is right, He will use you—but it's up to you to be thoroughly prepared when He does.

God gives His gifts where He finds the vessel
empty enough to receive them.

C. S. Lewis

God is the giver, and we are the receivers.
And His richest gifts are bestowed not upon
those who do the greatest things, but upon
those who accept His abundance and His grace.

Hannah Whitall Smith

We must stir up the gift of God.
Like sugar in the lemonade, it may be there,
but it needs to be set in motion.

Vance Havner

The Lord has abundantly blessed me all of
my life. I'm not trying to pay Him back for
all of His wonderful gifts; I just realize that
He gave them to me to give away.

Lisa Whelchel

As each one has received a gift,
minister it to one another,
as good stewards of the manifold grace of God.

1 Peter 4:10 NKJV

TODAY'S PRAYER

Lord, I praise You for Your priceless gifts.
I give thanks for Your creation, for Your Son,
and for the unique talents and opportunities
that You have given me. Let me use my gifts
for the glory of Your Kingdom,
this day and every day.
Amen

BIBLE VERSES TO CONSIDER

1 Corinthians 12:4-5; 1 Timothy 4:14;
2 Timothy 1:6; James 1:17

LIVING ABUNDANTLY

I have come that they may have life,
and that they may have it more abundantly.

John 10:10 NKJV

When Jesus talks of the abundant life, is He talking about material riches or earthly fame? Hardly. The Son of God came to this world, not to give it prosperity, but to give it salvation. Thankfully for Christians, our Savior's abundance is both spiritual and eternal; it never falters—even if we do—and it never dies. We need only to open our hearts to Him, and His grace becomes ours.

God's gifts are available to all, but they are not guaranteed; those gifts must be claimed by those who choose to follow Christ. As believers, we are free to accept God's gifts, or not; that choice, and the consequences that result from it, are ours and ours alone.

Do you sincerely seek the riches that our Savior offers to those who give themselves to Him? Then follow Him completely and obey Him without reservation. When you do, you will receive the love and the abundance that He has promised. Seek first the salvation that is available through a personal, passionate relationship with Christ, and then claim the joy, the peace, and the spiritual abundance that the Shepherd offers His sheep.

Jesus intended for us to be overwhelmed by the blessings of regular days. He said it was the reason he had come: "I am come that they might have life, and that they might have it more abundantly."

Gloria Gaither

God has promised us abundance, peace, and eternal life. These treasures are ours for the asking; all we must do is claim them. One of the great mysteries of life is why on earth do so many of us wait so very long to lay claim to God's gifts?

Marie T. Freeman

Jesus wants Life for us, Life with a capital L.

John Eldredge

If we were given all we wanted here, our hearts would settle for this world rather than the next.

Elisabeth Elliot

And God is able to make all grace abound to you,
so that always having all sufficiency in everything,
you may have an abundance for every good deed.

2 Corinthians 9:8 NASB

TODAY'S PRAYER

Thank You, Lord, for the abundant life given
through Your Son Jesus Christ. You have blessed
me beyond measure. Use me today and every
day to be a blessing to others so that I might
enthusiastically share Your abundance
with all who cross my path.
Amen

BIBLE VERSES TO CONSIDER

John 15:11; Luke 6:38; Matthew 13:12;
Matthew 25:21

SEEKING HIS KINGDOM

*But seek first the kingdom of God and
His righteousness, and all these things
shall be added to you.*

Matthew 6:33 NKJV

The familiar words of Matthew 6 remind us that, as believers, we must seek God and His kingdom. And when we seek Him with our hearts open and our prayers lifted, we need not look far: God is with us always.

Sometimes, however, in the crush of our daily duties, God may seem far away. But He is not. God is everywhere we have ever been and everywhere we will ever go. He is with us night and day; He knows our thoughts and our prayers. And, when we earnestly seek Him, we will find Him because He is here, waiting patiently for us to reach out to Him.

Today, let us reach out to the Giver of all blessings. Let us turn to Him for guidance and for strength. Today, may we, who have been given so much, seek God and invite Him into every aspect of our lives. And, let us remember that no matter our circumstances, God never leaves us; He is here . . . always right here.

As I contemplate all the sacrifices required in
order to live a life that is totally focused on
Jesus Christ and His eternal kingdom,
the joy seeps out of my heart onto my face
in a smile of deep satisfaction.

Anne Graham Lotz

Fasting helps to express, to deepen,
and to confirm the resolution that we are
ready to sacrifice anything—even to sacrifice
ourselves—to attain what we seek
for the kingdom of God.

Andrew Murray

What of the great prayer Jesus taught us to pray?
It is for His kingdom and His will,
yet we ought not to ask it unless we ourselves
are prepared to cooperate.

Elisabeth Elliot

Behold, the kingdom of God is within you.

Luke 17:21 KJV

TODAY'S PRAYER

How comforting it is, Dear Lord, to know that
if I diligently seek You and Your kingdom,
I will find You. You are with me, Father,
every step that I take. Let me reach out to You,
and let me praise You for revealing Your Word,
Your way, and Your love.
Amen

BIBLE VERSES TO CONSIDER

*Psalm 145:13; Matthew 6:9-10; Matthew 13:11;
Hebrews 12:28*

A PASSION
FOR WISDOM

Wisdom is a tree of life to those who embrace her;
happy are those who hold her tightly.

Proverbs 3:18 NLT

Wisdom is not like a dandelion; it does not spring up overnight. It is, instead, like an oak tree that starts as a tiny acorn, grows into a sapling, and eventually reaches up to the sky, tall and strong. To become wise, we must seek God's wisdom and live according to His Word. And, we must not only *learn* the lessons of the Christian life, we must also *live* by them.

Are you passionate in your pursuit of God's wisdom? And do you sincerely seek to live a life of righteousness? If so, you must study the ultimate source of wisdom: the Word of God. You must seek out worthy mentors and listen carefully to their advice. You must associate, day in and day out, with godly men and women. And, you must act in accordance with your beliefs. When you study God's Word and live according to His commandments, you will become wise . . . and you will be a blessing to your friends, to your family, and to the world.

Wisdom is knowledge applied.
Head knowledge is useless on the battlefield.
Knowledge stamped on the heart
makes one wise.

Beth Moore

Don't expect wisdom to come into
your life like great chunks of rock on
a conveyor belt. Wisdom comes privately
from God as a byproduct of right decisions,
godly reactions, and the application of
spiritual principles to daily circumstances.

Charles Swindoll

The fruit of wisdom is Christlikeness, peace,
humility, and love. And, the root of it is faith
in Christ as the manifested wisdom of God.

J. I. Packer

The more wisdom enters our hearts,
the more we will be able to trust our hearts
in difficult situations.

John Eldredge

*Those who are wise will shine like the brightness of
the heavens, and those who lead many
to righteousness, like the stars for ever and ever.*

Daniel 12:3 NIV

TODAY'S PRAYER

I seek wisdom, Lord, not as the world gives,
but as You give. Lead me in Your ways
and teach me from Your Word so that, in time,
my wisdom might glorify Your kingdom
and Your Son.
Amen

BIBLE VERSES TO CONSIDER

*Isaiah 50:4-5; James 1:5; Matthew 7:24;
Proverbs 1:5*

FOLLOWING
IN HIS
FOOTSTEPS

If anyone serves Me, let him follow Me;
and where I am, there My servant will be also.
If anyone serves Me, him My Father will honor.

John 12:26 NKJV

Jesus loved you so much that He endured unspeakable humiliation and suffering for you. How will you respond to Christ's sacrifice? Will you take up His cross and follow Him (Luke 9:23), or will you choose another path? When you place your hopes squarely at the foot of the cross, when you place Jesus squarely at the center of your life, you will be blessed.

The 19th-century writer Hannah Whitall Smith observed, "The crucial question for each of us is this: What do you think of Jesus, and do you yet have a personal acquaintance with Him?" Indeed, the answer to that question determines the quality, the course, and the direction of our lives today and for all eternity.

The old familiar hymn begins, "What a friend we have in Jesus . . . ." No truer words were ever penned. Jesus is the sovereign friend and ultimate savior of mankind. Christ showed enduring love for His believers by willingly sacrificing His own life so that we might have eternal life. Now, it is our turn to become His friend. And the very best moment to do so is this one.

When we truly walk with God throughout
our day, life slowly starts to fall into place.

Bill Hybels

Christ is like a river that is continually flowing.
There are always fresh supplies of water coming
from the fountain-head, so that a man may live
by it and be supplied with water all
his life. So Christ is an ever-flowing fountain;
he is continually supplying his people, and
the fountain is not spent. They who live upon
Christ may have fresh supplies from him
for all eternity; they may have an increase of
blessedness that is new, and new still,
and which never will come to an end.

Jonathan Edwards

A believer comes to Christ;
a disciple follows after Him.

Vance Havner

Then He said to them all, "If anyone wants to come with Me, he must deny himself, take up his cross daily, and follow Me."

Luke 9:23 HCSB

TODAY'S PRAYER

Dear Lord, You sent Your Son so that
I might have abundant life and eternal life.
Thank You, Father, for my Savior, Christ Jesus.
I will follow Him, honor Him, and share
His Good News, this day and every day.
Amen

BIBLE VERSES TO CONSIDER

*Romans 8:1; Matthew 10:38-39; Matthew 9:9;
Matthew 6:24*

NO GREATER LOVE

Greater love has no one than this,
that he lay down his life for his friends.

John 15:13 NIV

Where can we find God's love? Everywhere. God's love transcends space and time. It reaches beyond the heavens, and it touches the darkest, smallest corner of every human heart. When we become passionate in our devotion to the Father, when we sincerely open our minds and hearts to Him, His love does not arrive "some day"—it arrives immediately.

The words of Romans 8 make this promise: "For I am persuaded that neither death nor life, nor angels nor principalities nor powers, nor things present nor things to come, nor height nor depth, nor any other created thing, shall be able to separate us from the love of God which is in Christ Jesus our Lord" (38-39 NKJV).

Today, take God at His word and welcome His Son into your heart. When you do, God's transcendent love will surround you and transform you, now and forever.

God proved his love on the cross.
When Christ hung, and bled, and died it was
God saying to the world—I love you.

Billy Graham

The life of faith is a daily exploration of
the constant and countless ways in which
God's grace and love are experienced.

Eugene Peterson

God loves us the way we are,
but He loves us too much to leave us that way.

Leighton Ford

The spectacle of the Cross, the most public
event of Jesus' life, reveals the vast difference
between a god who proves himself
through power and One who proves
himself through love.

Philip Yancey

We love Him because He first loved us.

1 John 4:19 NKJV

TODAY'S PRAYER

God, You are love. I love You, Lord,
and as I love You more, I am able to show more
love to my family and friends. Let me be
Your loving servant, Heavenly Father,
today and throughout eternity.
Amen

BIBLE VERSES TO CONSIDER

*John 3:16; Lamentations 3:22; Psalm 100:4-5;
Romans 8:38-39*

MORE
BIBLE VERSES
TO CONSIDER

CELEBRATION

David and the whole house of Israel were
celebrating with all their might before the Lord,
with songs and with harps, lyres,
tambourines, sistrums and cymbals.

2 Samuel 6:5 NIV

This is the day which the Lord *has made;*
let us rejoice and be glad in it.

Psalm 118:24 NASB

At the dedication of the wall of Jerusalem,
the Levites were sought out from where they lived
and were brought to Jerusalem to celebrate joyfully
the dedication with songs of thanksgiving and
with the music of cymbals, harps and lyres.

Nehemiah 12:27 NIV

REJOICE IN THE LORD ALWAYS. I WILL SAY IT AGAIN: REJOICE!

Philippians 4:4 HCSB

COURAGE

But He said to them,
"Why are you fearful, you of little faith?"
Then He got up and rebuked the winds and the sea.
And there was a great calm.

Matthew 8:26 HCSB

The fear of man brings a snare,
but whoever trusts in the LORD shall be safe.

Proverbs 29:25 NKJV

Be of good courage, and He shall strengthen
your heart, all you who hope in the Lord.

Psalm 31:24 NKJV

I sought the LORD, and he answered me;
he delivered me from all my fears.

Psalm 34:4 NIV

ENTHUSIASM

*Never be lacking in zeal,
but keep your spiritual fervor, serving the Lord.*

Romans 12:11 NIV

He did it with all his heart, and prospered.

2 Chronicles 31:21 KJV

*Do your work with enthusiasm.
Work as if you were serving the Lord,
not as if you were serving only men and women.*

Ephesians 6:7 NCV

*O clap your hands, all peoples;
shout to God with the voice of joy.*

Psalm 47:1 NASB

THE GOOD NEWS

Sing to the LORD, *all the earth;*
proclaim the good news of His salvation
from day to day.

1 Chronicles 16:23 NKJV

But the angel said to them, "Do not be afraid,
for you see, I announce to you good news
of great joy that will be for all the people."

Luke 2:10 HCSB

The Spirit of the Lord is on me, because he has
anointed me to preach good news to the poor.
He has sent me to proclaim freedom for
the prisoners and recovery of sight for the blind,
to release the oppressed,
to proclaim the year of the Lord's favor.

Luke 4:18-19 NIV

For our gospel came not unto you in word only,
but also in power, and in the Holy Ghost,
and in much assurance . . . .

1 Thessalonians 1:5 KJV

AND THIS GOSPEL
OF THE KINGDOM
SHALL BE PREACHED
IN ALL THE WORLD
FOR A WITNESS
UNTO ALL NATIONS;
AND THEN SHALL
THE END COME.

Matthew 24:14 KJV

HOPE

This hope we have as an anchor of the soul,
a hope both sure and steadfast.

Hebrews 6:19 NASB

Happy is he who has the God of Jacob for his help,
whose hope is in the LORD his God.

Psalm 146:5 NKJV

May the God of hope fill you with all joy and
peace as you trust in him, so that you may overflow
with hope by the power of the Holy Spirit.

Romans 15:13 NIV

But if we hope for what we do not yet have,
we wait for it patiently.

Romans 8:25 NIV

I FIND REST IN GOD; ONLY HE GIVES ME HOPE.

Psalm 62:5 NCV

JESUS

I am the Vine, you are the branches.
When you're joined with me and I with you,
the relation intimate and organic,
the harvest is sure to be abundant.

John 15:5 MSG

Jesus answered, "I am the way and the truth and
the life. No one comes to the Father except through
me. If you really knew me, you would know
my Father as well. From now on,
you do know him and have seen him."

John 14:6-7 NIV

In the beginning was the Word, and the Word was
with God, and the Word was God . . . .
And the Word was made flesh, and dwelt among
us, (and we beheld his glory, the glory as of the only
begotten of the Father,) full of grace and truth.

John 1:1, 14 KJV

I AM THE DOOR.
IF ANYONE
ENTERS BY ME,
HE WILL BE SAVED.

—

John 10:9 NKJV

PRAYER

*And he withdrew himself into the wilderness,
and prayed.*

Luke 5:16 KJV

*Ask and it shall be given to you;
seek and you shall find; knock and it shall be
opened to you. For every one who asks receives,
and he who seeks finds, and to him who knocks
it shall be opened.*

Matthew 7:7-8 NASB

*In my distress I called upon the LORD;
I cried unto my God for help.
From his temple, he heard my voice.*

Psalm 18:6 NIV

*Let my prayer come before You;
incline Your ear to my cry!*

Psalm 88:2 NASB

THE EFFECTIVE PRAYER OF A RIGHTEOUS MAN CAN ACCOMPLISH MUCH.

—

James 5:16 NASB

OPTIMISM

*Finally, brethren, whatsoever things are true,
whatsoever things are honest, whatsoever things
are just, whatsoever things are pure,
whatsoever things are lovely, whatsoever things
are of good report; if there be any virtue,
and if there be any praise, think on these things.*

Philippians 4:8 KJV

*My cup runs over. Surely goodness and
mercy shall follow me all the days of my life;
and I will dwell in the house of the LORD Forever.*

Psalm 23:5-6 NKJV

*But we are hoping for something
we do not have yet,
and we are waiting for it patiently.*

Romans 8:25 NCV

I CAN DO EVERYTHING THROUGH HIM THAT GIVES ME STRENGTH.

—

Philippians 4:13 NIV

PURPOSE

There is one thing I always do.
Forgetting the past and straining toward what is
ahead, I keep trying to reach the goal and
get the prize for which God called me . . . .

Philippians 3:13-14 NCV

May He grant you according to your heart's desire,
and fulfill all your purpose.

Psalm 20:4 NKJV

God chose you to be his people,
so I urge you now to live the life
to which God called you.

Ephesians 4:1 NCV

You will show me the path of life;
in Your presence is fullness of joy;
at Your right hand are pleasures forevermore.

Psalm 16:11 NKJV

TO EVERYTHING THERE IS A SEASON, A TIME FOR EVERY PURPOSE UNDER HEAVEN.

—

Ecclesiastes 3:1 NKJV

JOY

Let the hearts of those who seek the Lord rejoice.
Look to the Lord and his strength;
seek his face always.

1 Chronicles 16:10-11 NIV

These things I have spoken to you,
that My joy may remain in you,
and that your joy may be full.

John 15:11 NKJV

Rejoice, and be exceeding glad:
for great is your reward in heaven . . . .

Matthew 5:12 KJV

Weeping may remain for a night,
but rejoicing comes in the morning.

Psalm 30:5 NIV

MAKE ME HEAR JOY AND GLADNESS.

—

Psalm 51:8 NKJV

GOD'S PLANS

"For I know the plans I have for you,"
declares the Lord, "plans to prosper you and
not to harm you, plans to give you hope and
a future. Then you will call upon me and come
and pray to me, and I will listen to you."

Jeremiah 29:11-12 NIV

People may make plans in their minds,
but the LORD decides what they will do.

Proverbs 16:9 NCV

There is no wisdom, no insight,
no plan that can succeed against the LORD.

Proverbs 21:30 NIV

We know that all things work together for
the good of those who love God:
those who are called according to His purpose.

Romans 8:28 HCSB

IT IS GOD WHO IS AT WORK IN YOU, BOTH TO WILL AND TO WORK FOR HIS GOOD PLEASURE.

—

Philippians 2:13 NASB

CHRIST'S LOVE

Who will separate us from the love of Christ?
Will tribulation, or distress, or persecution,
or famine, or nakedness, or peril, or sword? . . .
But in all these things we overwhelmingly conquer
through Him who loved us.

Romans 8:35, 37 NASB

For I am convinced that neither death, nor life,
nor angels, nor principalities, nor things present,
nor things to come, nor powers, nor height,
nor depth, nor any other created thing,
will be able to separate us from the love of God,
which is in Christ Jesus our Lord.

Romans 8:38-39 NASB

Just as the Father has loved Me,
I have also loved you; abide in My love.

John 15:9 NASB

I AM THE GOOD SHEPHERD. THE GOOD SHEPHERD LAYS DOWN HIS LIFE FOR THE SHEEP.

—

John 10:11 NIV

JESUS CHRIST IS THE SAME YESTERDAY AND TODAY AND FOREVER.

Hebrews 13:8 NASB